Who is Chosen?

Who is Chosen?

Four Theories about Christian Salvation

THOMAS L. HUMPHRIES, JR.

WIPF & STOCK · Eugene, Oregon

Wipf & Stock
An Imprint of Wipf and Stock Publishers
199 W. 8th Ave., Suite 3
Eugene, OR 97401

www.wipfandstock.com

PAPERBACK ISBN: 978-1-5326-3217-4
HARDCOVER ISBN: 978-1-5326-3219-8
EBOOK ISBN: 978-1-5326-3218-1

Manufactured in the U.S.A.   JUNE 9, 2017

This work is dedicated to
my fellow students and teachers of salvation.

Contents

Contents

Acknowledgments

Profound thanks are owed to my mentors and my colleagues. Peter Casarella was the first to introduce me to eschatology as a proper theological discipline focused on the virtue of hope. Lewis Ayres did quite a bit more than introduce me to St. Augustine! Steve Okey, Lily Abadal, Christine Humphries, and Dan Lloyd read copies of this manuscript and offered helpful criticism and suggestions. Life on campus near the monks of Saint Leo Abbey and the students helped to keep me prayerfully focused. Life at home has been wonderfully blessed by my wife (who understands the time needed to write even a short book) and our newborn daughter (who "understands" the need for frequent breaks).

Introduction

To be Christian is to accept in faith, hope, and love that Jesus Christ is the "way, and the truth, and the life."[1] That is, the Word of God Incarnate offers salvation to mankind. This is a fundamental belief for Christians. Indeed, there seem to be few other reasons for one to be Christian than to suppose that being a true disciple of Christ is the only way to salvation. Acts 4:12 makes the point succinctly: "There is no salvation through anyone else, nor is there any other name under heaven given to the human race by which we are to be saved." Furthermore, one belongs to Christ in the body of salvation through the Church. This mystery of salvation is part of the mystery of the Trinity, and together with it, defines Christianity. The fourth century creeds profess belief in the Father, the Son, the Holy Spirit, and the Church. Christianity alone is the means to forgiveness of sins and redemption.

There are many who would question the exclusivity of Christianity as the path to salvation. Those who are not Christian, of course, have a different belief. But even some within Christianity question whether Christ is the only Savior. A more acute form of this line of questioning focuses on whether Christ could save those who do not somehow belong to God through the Church,

---

1. John 14:6. All Scripture translations are taken from the New American Bible, unless otherwise noted.

or whether Christ could save those who do not explicitly identify with him but accept other aspects of truth and goodness under a different name. Those are complex questions that deserve careful consideration. They, however, are not the focus of this short book. Here, I want to present four theories that all intend to be firmly Christian in the sense that they all assume that Christ is the only way to salvation and that the plan of salvation is worked out by the Triune God.

This book presents four key theologians who are fountainheads of distinct schools of thought. It argues that each is a distinct school of thought based on the way it addresses a fundamental problem presented in the Christian Scriptures. God seems to reveal in Scripture two contradictory claims. On the one hand, it appears that God wants all to be saved and will ultimately succeed in establishing that reality. On the other hand, it appears that some or even many have already definitively rejected God and arrived in a Hell that is not only real, but already over-populated. In the face of this basic exegetical problem, we are tempted to take one principle as foundational and use it to correct or understand the others. We may take the idea that all will be saved as the fundamental truth and follow Origen in speculating that Hell could be real, while also rejecting an eternal damnation that mirrors eternal salvation. We may take the idea that some will end up in an eternal Hell and follow Augustine in attempting to defend that God is still good and powerful. We may take the same assumption that some or even many will end up in an eternal Hell and follow Calvin in arguing that God's greater glory is served by admitting that God's will is absolute and always just, even if we are created as vessels of perdition. Finally, we may reject the premise that one set of Scripture verses must be accepted as more fundamental and follow Balthasar in reflecting on what remains for hope. The intention of the book is not to argue that one theory is better than another, but to help the interested student in hopes that she may make a better and more informed decision in her own faith. Those who wish to study more should first consult the primary texts referenced in the notes.

1

Christian Salvation in Sacred Scripture

OUR GOD IS A saving God. Christianity shares this faith in a God who saves with Judaism, for God tells us, "I, the LORD, am your God who brought you out of the land of Egypt, that place of slavery."[1] Moreover, for Christians, the history of salvation culminates in Jesus Christ. In the Incarnation of the Word, the Second Person of the Trinity, God definitively reveals himself as Savior. If we think of the "Old" Covenant at Mount Sinai and the "New" Covenant at the Last Supper, we see bookends to the dramatic way God acts in history to bring about salvation for his people. In fact, salvation was the lynchpin for many of the most significant debates in early Christian theology. When theologians wanted to judge a theory about Jesus Christ or about the church, they would ask whether it resonated with Scripture to reveal that Jesus offers salvation. Any picture of Jesus that made him less than the Savior and any picture of the church that made her less than the mechanism of salvation were rejected. One joins the church because it is the way, the truth, and the life which leads to salvation.

The deeds of salvation history are recounted through the words of sacred Scripture. God has a "message" for us. But that

1. Deut 5:6. All Scripture translations are taken from the New American Bible, unless otherwise noted.

"message" is not always easy to understand. In his infinite mercy, God creates us and loves us (Gen 1–2). But we turn away from God and bring punishment on ourselves (Gen 3). Everything in Scripture after Genesis 3 is tainted with human sinfulness, and yet, our original goodness and God's fundamental love for us continue to be seen. God establishes a covenant with his people through Noah (Gen 9) and through Abraham (Gen 17). God saves his people from Egyptian bondage (esp. Ex 12–14) and forms a covenant with us on Mt. Sinai (Ex 19–20). The covenant continues through the line of David to Jesus Christ, who offers his own blood as part of the New Covenant (Mt 26:27–28). The New Covenant in Jesus' own blood is universal. "For just as in Adam all die, so too in Christ shall all be brought to life . . . For he must reign until he has put all his enemies under his feet."[2] God "wills everyone to be saved and to come to the knowledge of the truth."[3] Jesus is relevant for *every* human being. God is Creator of *all* mankind. And yet, God loves Jacob and hates Esau (Mal 1:3, Rom 9:13). There is one kind of judgment that leads to the Kingdom and another kind of judgment that leads into the eternal fire (Mt 25:31–46). The path to destruction is wide, and the way that leads to life is narrow (Mt 7:13–14). God clearly has a plan to save his people, but it is not clear whether his people includes some but not others or whether everyone will be brought to life in Jesus Christ. St. Luke recounts that "Someone asked him, 'Lord, will only a few people be saved?' He answered them, 'Strive to enter through the narrow gate, for many, I tell you, will attempt to enter but will not be strong enough.'"[4] But St. John tells us that Jesus said, "And when I am lifted up from the earth, I will draw everyone to myself."[5] The story of salvation is not a simple one that follows a straight line.

> Christianity is about salvation!

2. 1 Cor 15.22–25.
3. 1 Tim 2:4.
4. Luke 13:23–24.
5. John 12:32.

OVERVIEW OF SALVATION HISTORY

It is important to remember who some of the key figures in the story of salvation are and how that history is told. Catholics believe that God writes the story of salvation first in the hearts and lives of real human beings. That story is then recorded and told to generation after generation in the inspired texts of Sacred Scripture. This means that we have to think about the original human lives as they unfold as well as the way the story is told if we want to read the narrative of salvation well. Adam and Eve, as the first man and woman, stand as the "parents" or "founders" for all of humanity. It is common to think not only of these individuals, but of the entire human race wrapped up in this first couple. "Adam" can stand for all males or even all human beings. Eve can stand for all women. Together, they represent all of humanity from the very beginning. St. Paul plays with these characters and themes when he observes that Jesus is the "new Adam" or the "second Adam."[6] Adam and Eve had three sons, Abel, Cain, and Seth. Cain killed Abel (Gen 4). With Abel murdered and Cain the murderer, Adam and Eve's family lineage is traced through Seth all the way to Noah (Gen 5). Noah built the Ark and weathered the storm that lasted "forty days and forty nights" (Gen 6–7). When the waters finally receded several months later, God formed a covenant with Noah, the sign of which is the rainbow (Gen 9). Noah fathered three sons, Shem, Ham, and Japheth. Ham's line established the ancient people of Canaan.[7] Shem's line included Abraham.[8] Thus, we see that the house of Abraham was distantly related to the people of Canaan. There is a curious story about Noah getting drunk and laying nude in his tent. His three sons find him, but two look away and cover Noah while Ham (inappropriately) looked at his father.[9] This explains why it was legitimate for Abraham (in the line of Shem) to take the land of Canaan. Ham's sin, just like Adam and Eve's sin, affected

6. For example, see 1 Cor 15:45–49 and Rom 5:12–21.

7. Gen 9:18.

8. Gen 11:10–26.

9. Gen 9:20–27.

his descendants. The case is similar between Abraham's sons Ishmael and Isaac. Abraham and Sarah were promised descendants as numerous as the stars in the sky, but they were unable to conceive a child for quite some time.[10] Sarah gave her servant, Hagar, to Abraham in order to produce a child, and Abraham fathered Ishmael with Hagar (Gen 16). But Hagar and Ishmael were not the way God intended to bless Abraham in the line of the covenant. Miraculously, Sarah and Abraham conceived after she had entered menopause, and they named their son Isaac (Gen 17). God continued his covenant with Isaac, who bore Abraham's lineage; Ishmael and Hagar were banished from Abraham's land and lost any inheritance (Gen 21). Here again it is possible to see that Abraham and Hagar made a mistake in following Sarah's initial judgment that they should attempt to fulfil God's promise of descendants on their own. Ishmael and his mother bear the punishment. Muslims trace their lineage through Ishmael, but also think that he was a favored son. Jews follow the line of Isaac. That storyline changes rationale with Isaac's sons, Esau and Jacob.

Like his parents, Isaac and Rebekah were sterile and conceived in part by God's miraculous intervention. Rebekah became pregnant with the twins Esau and Jacob (Gen 25). Esau was born first, but Jacob was born "gripping Esau's heel."[11] In effect, the two were born at the same time. As many would later argue, this is significant because there are no grounds upon which to distinguish the new–born Esau from his new–born brother, Jacob. For example, Augustine argues against the premise of astrology by noting that the two should have had the same fortune, since they were born under identical astrological conditions.[12] But this also presents a shift in the way we think about salvation history. To think of only the men, we could note that the lines of Adam-Cain, Noah-Ham, and Abraham-Ishmael are all punished for their ancestor's sins. Cain, Ham, and Ishmael present the character of the "bad brother," and we can find human reasons to blame them. They are

10. Gen 15:2–5.
11. Gen 25:26.
12. Augustine, *Confessions* 7.6.8–7.6.10.

responsible in some way for their troubles. With Esau and Jacob, even before their birth, God seems to favor one over the other. God tells Rebekah, "Two peoples are quarrelling while still within you; but one shall surpass the other, and the older shall serve the younger."[13] Jacob takes the birthright from his elder brother and becomes the favored son.[14] Jacob's twelve sons became the fathers of the twelve tribes of Israel, while Esau married into the Canaanite line and fathered the Edomites.[15] Jacob and Esau, the twins, are presented according to a standard pattern of God's choice resting with one and not the other brother. However, God's choice does not seem to be based on Jacob and Esau's actions, but rather on God's own decision. Thus, the prophet Malachi proclaims God's word to Israel, "I loved Jacob, but hated Esau."[16]

Abbreviated Genealogy of Salvation History			
	Adam & Eve		
Abel	Cain	**Seth**	
		Noah	
	Shem	Ham	Japheth
Sarah—Abraham—Hagar		*Canaanites*	
Isaac	Ishmael		
Jacob	Esau		
Israelites	*Edomites*		
Moses			
David			
Jesus			

Moses is born of the house of Levi, from Jacob's descendants. God identifies himself to Moses as "the God of your father . . . the

13. Gen 25:23.

14. See Gen 25:31–33 & Gen 27:1–29.

15. See Gen 35:22–26, Gen 36, and Gen 49.

16. Mal 1:3.

God of Abraham, the God of Isaac, the God of Jacob."[17] God is not revealed as the God of Ishmael and the God of Esau. God forms a new covenant with Moses that ratifies and, in effect, updates the covenant made with Noah and Abraham. The covenant with Moses is made at Mount Sinai (also called "Horeb") and includes the famous Ten Commandments as well as many other laws.[18] Another famous "son" in the line of Jacob is King David in the house of Judah.[19] God renews his promise to the Israelite people through David as their King: "Your house and your kingdom shall endure forever before me; your throne shall stand firm forever."[20] St. Matthew notes the significance of these family relationships when he calls Jesus the "son of David, the son of Abraham."[21] Though scholars sometimes argue that "many" is a colloquial term that does not exclude everyone, it does at least appear that even Jesus admits that some, but not all, will belong to God under Jesus' "blood of the covenant which will be shed on behalf of many for the forgiveness of sins."[22] Many of the stories in the Old Testament explain why *these* people belong in a special way to God but *those* people do not. At times, it appears that those who do not belong are somewhat to blame (e.g. Ham and the Canaanites for not treating Noah appropriately). At other times, it appears that God simply chooses one over the other (e.g. Jacob and Esau). Even as the Savior with universal significance, Jesus himself allows for the interpretation that many, but not all, will be saved.

AN "EXEGETICAL PROBLEM"

Sacred Scripture certainly leaves open the possibility that God saves some, but not all humans. In places, damnation seems to be

17. Exod 3:6.
18. See Ex. 19–20 & Deut 5.
19. 1 Chr 2:1–15.
20. 2 Sam 7:16.
21. Matt 1:1.
22. Matt 26:28.

punishment for our past sins or the sins of our ancestors. In other places, it almost appears that damnation is caused directly by the will of God before we are born. Scripture also seems to speak in different ways about the requirements for attaining salvation. In places, Scripture suggests that we are more or less responsible for our own destiny, but in other places, Scripture suggests that we have very little to do with the final outcome of our lives. In the New Testament, Peter tells us, "be all the more eager to make your call and election firm, for, in doing so, you will never stumble. For, in this way, entry into the eternal kingdom of our Lord and Savior Jesus Christ will be richly provided for you."[23] Matthew tells us, "Whoever believes and is baptized will be saved; whoever does not believe will be condemned."[24] But Paul suggests salvation has more to do with God's predestination than our eagerness or being baptized: "And those he predestined he also called; and those he called he also justified; and those he justified he also glorified."[25] This raises a problem for Christians who want to be sensitive to Scripture and develop a consistent theory or picture of how salvation works. Not only is the number of those saved not clear (i.e. "all," "many," or only "a few"), but the criteria listed seem contradictory (i.e. is it something humans do or something God does?). While Sacred Scripture is the "word of God," it does not seem to speak with a consistent voice.

Since the problem of how many are saved and for what reason they are saved presents us as we read Scripture, we call this an "exegetical problem." The problem arises directly from reading Scripture. In all honesty, the first solution that most often presents itself is to ignore the verses that do not resonate with us. However, this is not a satisfactory solution. It would lead to broadly different understandings of the plan of salvation, and the plan of salvation is central to Christianity. Furthermore, we expect God to have a consistent plan of salvation that is revealed in Sacred Scripture. Theologians are stuck between a rock and a hard place. We can either

23. 2 Pet 1:10–11.
24. Matt 16:16.
25. Rom 8:30.

give up on finding the truth within Scripture or we can give up on the "meat" of the Faith, which is salvation. Some of the most intelligent and holy theologians have attempted to solve this exegetical problem. Three basic strategies have presented themselves within Christianity. The first is to argue that God has always chosen some and not others. This requires an awkward reading of passages like "This is good and pleasing to God our savior, who wills everyone to be saved and to come to knowledge of the truth."[26] "Everyone" does not mean "each and every," but *only* those who are not damned. A second strategy is to read passages like "in Christ . . . all [shall] be brought to life . . . For he must reign until he has put all enemies under his feet," to mean that God will eventually "win" and all humans will come to follow him and enjoy him in Heaven.[27] But then when God loves Jacob and hates Esau, God's "hate" cannot mean eternal damnation, but somehow God's plan for redemption.[28] It can be confusing to think both of God's love and God's hate as the same plan for redemption. Furthermore, this seems to deny genuine human freedom since everyone would end up in Heaven regardless of how they lived. A third strategy is to argue that because Scripture presents evidence that seems conflicting, God does not want us to know exactly how this works. How many are saved is not a matter of *faith* such that to be Christian is to believe that this many or that many are saved; rather, to be Christian is to *hope* that God meaningfully offers salvation to all and allows everyone genuine freedom to love.[29]

> *Exegesis* means discerning the meaning of a Scripture passage. Scholars use several tools to help this process including history, archaeology, context, and prayer.

Tracking theories of salvation as responses to an exegetical problem has definite benefits. It offers us a particular lens through which to read nearly two thousand years of dense theological

26. 1 Tim 2:3–4. This is generally Augustine's strategy.

27. 1 Cor 15:22–25. This is generally Origen's strategy.

28. Mal 1:1–3 and Rom 9:13–14.

29. This is generally Hans Urs von Balthasar's strategy.

reflection. It also allows us to compare various theologians under a relatively simple and clear set of criteria. We can select a small handful of verses and see how different theologians treat those verses. Treating the problem of salvation solely as an exegetical problem also has downfalls. It could blind us to the lived experience of Christians after the New Testament was written, and it could lead us away from the complicated, but carefully articulated philosophical and theological concerns, like whether the freedom and power of God is somehow at odds with the freedom and power of humans. Focusing only on the exegetical problem could also allow us to ignore the formal history of interpretation offered by the Magisterium (the formal teaching authority) of the Church, for example, with decisions made at Ecumenical Councils. Scripture is a fundamental part of theology, even if not the only thing to take into consideration. In this book, we will focus on four different exegetical strategies in order to study theories of Christian salvation.

> Christians have used an *Ecumenical Council,* a gathering of bishops from around the world, to make authoritative decisions about significant theological and practical issues.

2

Origenism and
the Restoration of All Things

ORIGEN OF ALEXANDRIA (185–232 AD) is one of the most influential and controversial theologians. Many of his ideas were called
into question by various theologians, eventually leading to a formal
condemnation by the Ecumenical Council which met in Constantinople in 553, three centuries after his death. Even within his own
lifetime he was subject to personal scrutiny from his bishop in Alexandria, Demetrius, though he was acclaimed as a solid theologian in
other regions. His father, Leonides, was martyred for the Faith, and
Origen came close to the same fate.[1] Though controversial, Origen
was a powerful teacher and writer. He was one of the first Christians to explore what it means that we use various versions, editions,
and translations of Scripture. He laid out distinct versions of the
Old Testament, presenting six different versions (Hebrew, Hebrew
transliterated into Greek, and four alternative Greek versions) on a
single page in what we call the *Hexapla*. How to interpret Scripture
correctly was often the focus of his theology. He also explored many
other difficult theological topics and thus, in one way or another, is
the fountainhead of a great deal of Christian theology. Origen was
quite willing to entertain the notion that everyone could eventually

1. For details on Origen's life, see Eusebius, *History of the Church* 6.1–6.3.
The rest of that chapter details Origen's works.

return to God, but he cautioned that this was "discussion rather than . . . definition."[2] In terms of theories of salvation, then, Origen is associated with "Universalism," the thesis that every human person will eventually be saved.

Origen's theological framework is premised on his doctrine of God. God is good and powerful. God is also the Creator of the universe. "All things that exist were made by God . . . who is good by nature."[3] There is a deep sense in Origen's thought that the end will be parallel to the beginning. A single good beginning (i.e. God creating the world) implies a single good end (i.e. Heaven). To put it another way, if God is ultimately all–powerful and all–good, there is no human power that can defeat God. The lines of Psalm 139 resonated deeply with Origen: "Where can I hide from your spirit? From your presence, where can I flee? If I ascend to the heavens, you are there; if I lie down in Sheol, you are there, too."[4] There is nowhere we can hide from God. For Origen, it makes sense to consider that God will eventually win, and no matter how much we might resist God, we will eventually come to see his truth. It is helpful to think of the image of an athletic team in which the coach sets the goal that everyone will run a mile before leaving school. Some sprint full speed in a straight path towards the finish line. Others take a slower, meandering path. Still others might turn around and run the other direction simply to spite the coach. But, by the end of the day, everyone will eventually cross the finish line. For Origen, God is like the coach, only God will never let an athlete walk away from the race. God will ensure that everyone finishes. Since God is eternal, we cannot simply wait for him to fade away or forget the race. God

> *Universalism* refers to something that applies to everyone. In the context of a theory of salvation it means "everyone will be saved."

is all–powerful, so we cannot simply resist him. God is good, so we cannot expect to sneak past the finish line with even a modicum of sin. God eventually converts even the most wretched sinner.

2. Origen, *On First Principles* 1.6.1, trans. Butterworth, 52.

3. Origen, *On First Principles* 4.4.8, trans. Butterworth, 323.

4. Ps 139:7–8.

THE EXEGETICAL ARGUMENT FOR UNIVERSALISM

Origen premises his speculation on a set of Scripture verses from the New Testament that begins with 1 Cor 15:25–27: "For [Christ] must reign until he has put all his enemies under his feet. The last enemy to be destroyed is death, for 'he subjected everything under his feet.'" Origen argues that "the word subjection, when used of our subjection to Christ, implies the salvation, proceeding from Christ, of those who are subject."[5] The point is simple. Christ will reign until he has defeated the very last enemy. But in Origen's understanding of the passage, "defeat of his enemies" implies that Christ saves his enemies. There will be no more evil when Christ reigns over the entire universe in glory. The Letter to the Philippians makes the same point in the Christological Hymn: Christ has the "name that is above every name . . . at the name of Jesus every knee should bend, of those in heaven and on the earth and under the earth."[6] Furthermore, "every tongue [will] confess that Jesus Christ is Lord."[7] Even those who do not profess Jesus right now will eventually profess Jesus' name; they will eventually bend their knees and be subject to Christ. To be subject to Christ is to have Christ as your Savior. Thus, Origen speculates that "the goodness of God through Christ will restore his entire creation to one end, even his enemies being conquered and subdued."[8]

THE GOOD GOD WHO IS BEGINNING AND END

Origen entertains the idea that everything comes from and returns to the one source of good (i.e. God): "The end is always like the beginning . . . there is one beginning of all things . . . and . . . one end . . . so from one beginning arise many differences and varieties,

---

5. Origen, On First Principles 1.6.1, trans. Butterworth, 52–53.

6. Phil. 2:9–10.

7. Phil. 2:11.

8. Origen, On First Principles 1.6.1, trans. Butterworth, 52.

which in their turn are restored through God's goodness."[9] Even though Origen is explicit that he writes about this topic only with "fear and caution, discussing and investigating rather than laying down fixed and certain conclusions," it is easy to think that his position on universal salvation has denied human freedom.[10] If everyone makes it to Heaven, we appear to be stuck with two alternatives: either (1) It does not matter what anyone does, or (2) we are not truly free to choose any alternative to Heaven. Christian theologians do not want to deny human free will; nor do we want to devalue human actions and their consequences. Origen is aware of these problems and works to resolve them. Origen teaches that we do have freedom and it does matter what humans do. Those who sin have farther to go in their return to God. God does not simply accept the sinner and place him in Heaven. Rather, God is patient and powerful. God turns the sinner around and accompanies her all the way back to the heart of goodness, no matter how far she has moved away from God. Because Origen thinks this springs from God's nature and applies to all of creation, he has to consider whether the same eventual restoration applies not only to humans, but also to fallen angels. True to the speculative project, Origen leaves the question open: "Whether . . . those [who] . . . live under the chieftainship of the devil . . . will one day in the ages to come succeed in turning to goodness by reason of the power of free–will . . . or whether it be true that long–continued and deep–rooted wickedness turns at last from a habit into a kind of nature, you, reader, must judge."[11]

It is important to note that Origen's argument does not proceed from a God who is supremely nice. We are tempted to think of God that way today, as if God looks the other way while sinners sneak through the pearly gates and into Heaven. There is no "extra credit" in Origen's system. No excuses are made for those who sin. People get what they deserve. God, however, does not provide eternal judgment for temporal mistakes. Rather, God works with

9. Origen, *On First Principles* 1.6.2, trans. Butterworth, 53.

10. Origen, *On First Principles* 1.6.1, trans. Butterworth, 52.

11. Origen, *On First Principles* 1.6.3, trans. Butterworth, 56–57.

everyone until she deserves Heaven. To return to the image of crossing the finish line, when God finds some have completed the race quickly, others may be close, and still others may be miles away, God works with each differently. God's actions will include restoring everyone. The malcontent who ran miles in the opposite direction does not stop there without finishing the race, but rather, must turn around and run back in the other direction. It will be much more difficult for the malcontent, for he will have to make up for going the wrong direction, but he will eventually turn around and run through the finish line. God will bring this about. For some, arriving in Heaven will be easy and relatively quick. For others, arriving in Heaven could mean passing through Hell. But passing through Hell is really just taking the "long road" to Heaven. Hell is not a definitive state of punishment and separation from God, but rather a finite state of remediation so that we eventually end up with God in Heaven. In this way Origen's sense of Hell corresponds to Purgatory. When Scripture teaches that "God is a consuming fire," or that God is like a refiner who uses fire to purify, this means that God will purify every sinner.[12] The fires of Hell are not punishment so much as they are refinement and purification.

> Origen speculates that Hell is remediation for sins, and therefore not eternal.

THE PROBLEM OF EVIL

If everyone starts from a good beginning and returns to that same good end, it is difficult to explain why anyone would meander away from the beginning. It is also very difficult to explain why an all–good God would create an order that includes diversity and variety to the point of pain and suffering. Why must one creature live at the expense of another, as when a lion must kill a zebra to survive? Why are some people born into immense wealth with loving families, but others are born into abject poverty with no

---

12. Deut 4:24, Heb 12:9, and Zech 13:9.

support? These questions follow the general line of thought that is part of the "problem of evil." It seems impossible that an all–powerful and all–good God could create a world in which there is pain, suffering, and evil. Origen's basic answer to this problem is that rational creatures have a free will and have used it poorly. We are responsible for our own bad situations. The fundamental scriptural reference for this is Genesis 3, where we learn about the Fall of Adam and Eve. But Origen has a unique and complicated understanding of how this Fall plays out in creation. For Origen, free will explains not only the problem of evil, but also what we might call the "problem of natural diversity." The problem of natural diversity considers questions like why one person is born blind when most are not, or why some are born in a worse social or economic situation in life than others. Natural diversity appears to set some up for failure; the child of parents addicted to drugs seems to have less of a chance to succeed than the child born to parents not addicted to drugs. Origen seems to envision a kind of two–stage creation.[13] First, God created rational beings (aka "souls") with free will. Then, God asked each rational being how close it wanted to remain to him, or what kind of thing it wanted to be. Some rational beings wanted to remain very close to God, and so, wanted to be angels of the highest order. Other rational beings wanted some separation from God, and so, chose to be humans. Other rational beings wanted to be farther from God, and so, chose to be other animals. As a second stage of creation, God then honors each soul's decision and completes creation. In this way, we are all responsible for our particular lot in life, even if we do not remember that prior decision. Origen references this theory when discussing Jacob and Esau: "we believe that by reason of his merits in some previous life Jacob had deserved to be loved by God to such an extent as to be worthy of being preferred to his brother."[14] The

---

13. See Origen, *On First Principles* 1.4.1. This "Fall" is linked to a Platonic decent into materiality and was the subject of intense critique by later Christian theologians. Bodies are not punishment for prior immaterial decisions according to Christian teaching, though Origen seems comfortable with that idea.

14. Origen, *On First Principles* 2.9.7, trans. Butterworth, 135.

"previous life" here does not appeal to some kind of re-incarnation, but rather some fundamental choice that the souls of Jacob and Esau made at the moment God created them. Esau, then, is not blindly punished at the random whim of God. Nor is Jacob unfairly favored by God. Esau has chosen a path that leads farther away from God and perhaps even leads to Hell. Nevertheless, God will not leave Esau in Hell. Esau will simply have a more difficult path to Heaven. When God hates Esau, he truly "hates the sin, and not the sinner," as the phrase goes. God's hate takes the form of remediation, not retribution, according to Origen.

> The *problem of evil* notes that the existence of evil is incompatible with the existence of a God who is both all-good and all-powerful. The *problem of natural diversity* notes that it is difficult to explain why an all-good and all-powerful God would create some things as less than others.

KEY QUESTIONS

It is helpful to pose a series of questions about Christian theories of salvation in order to compare various theologians. "Who is responsible for salvation and damnation?" and "how many people enter Heaven?" are key questions to consider. For Origen, humans are directly responsible not only for our present sins, but also for that initial or original sin that landed us where we find ourselves at the beginning of life in this world. Thus, human free will responds to both the problem of evil and the problem of natural diversity for Origen. In both cases, Origen thinks that individual rational beings (angels and humans are included in his theory) are responsible; God is not responsible for evil in any sense. In parallel fashion, those who return to God are definitely aided by God, but they make a free choice to return to God. For some creatures, God does not have to persuade them much to return to him. For others, God may have to use the pain of Hell to persuade them to return, but eventually, it seems that God will convince every rational creature to return to him and live in the redeemed joy of Heaven.

Other questions that are worth reflection and discussion include:

- If "every knee shall bend, and every tongue confess that Jesus is Lord," summarizes God's plan for salvation, what does this mean for sinful Christians? What does it imply for those who are decent people, but not Christians?

- Would it necessarily deny human free will if everyone ended up in Heaven?

- Why should Christians think Hell is everlasting punishment instead of finite remediation?

A SHORT CRITIQUE OF ORIGEN

There are longstanding historical critiques of Origen on salvation, and it is beneficial to review a few of them. Though there is some debate about the exact date of the particular anathemas against Origen, it is clear that the Council of Constantinople in 553 considered Origen heretical, even if the specifics are not discussed explicitly. He is remembered by later councils in 681 AD and in 787 AD as a heretic. The anathemas against Origen that date from the seventh century raise significant critiques of his theory of salvation. First, pre–existent souls are found to be problematic. This denies Origen's mechanism for explaining natural diversity and the pain, suffering, and evil wrapped up with it by appeal to creaturely free will. Origen needs pre–existent souls in order to say that those souls are responsible for their lower state in life, as with Esau. Without the pre–existent soul that allows Esau to have chosen poorly before his birth, God appears to hate Esau on a flimsy divine whim. Secondly, Christians come specifically to reject the teaching that "all reasonable beings will one day be united in one" single restoration.[15] This seems to deny human free will by closing the possibility of human failure. Other collections of anathemas

15. This language is found in the fifteenth of the fifteen anathemas against Origen. The translation comes from the Nicene and Post Nicene Fathers 2.14.319.

also condemn the notion that Hell is finite or temporal.[16] Many take it as revealed in Scripture that Hell is everlasting punishment, and that there is no escape from Hell. These are serious critiques. If the punishment of Hell is everlasting, then Origen's speculation that people go to Hell in order to convert cannot be correct. If Christians definitively deny that everyone could be saved, then Origen's speculation must be set aside.

16. E.g., the nine anathemas of the Emperor Justinian against Origen, translated in NPNF 2.14.320.

3

St. Augustine of Hippo

ST. AUGUSTINE (D. 430) was born to a pagan father and a Catholic mother in northern Africa (modern Algeria) in 354. He is revered as a Saint and a Doctor of the Church today, and his feast is celebrated on 28 August, the day after the feast of his mother, St. Monica. Though his family considered having him baptized at an early age, his baptism was deferred. In his *Confessions*, Augustine explores the various ways in which God was leading him to the Catholic Church, even when Augustine tried to find satisfaction in other religions, various philosophies, and different pleasures of this world. He analyzes his own experience mostly in terms of lust and pride. He traveled to Carthage, Rome, and Milan, where he was eventually baptized as an adult by St. Ambrose, though infant baptism was common in his day. He became a monk of sorts, returned to north Africa, and was then recruited as the bishop of a small town (Hippo) near his home. Over the course of his career he not only wrote extensively about many important theological topics, but he also changed his mind about how best to understand the human situation. Of particular relevance for his theory of salvation are his teachings about original sin (from Genesis 3) and his teachings about divine grace, human free will, and God's plan of salvation (largely from Paul's letters).

As a mature theologian, Augustine argued that humans are broken on multiple levels. Augustine found it convenient to think of three major layers of human existence: knowledge, love, and action. Based on his reflection on his own life, his pastoral experience, and his study of Scripture, Augustine argues that every human finds herself conflicted about knowing what is good and right. To follow Augustine's basic position, we should simply ask ourselves, "Have I ever not known what the right thing or good thing to do is?" Augustine thinks we will all answer, "yes!" This is because our knowledge is not perfect. We have broken minds. Similarly, even when we know the good, Augustine argues that we will not always choose the good. Augustine has real insight into humanity at this level; he always argues that choice and love are related. To love something or someone is to choose that object or person. If the epitome of the mind is knowledge of truth, then the epitome of the will is love. To follow Augustine's basic position about the broken human will, we should ask ourselves, "Have I ever known what was right, but not chosen to do it?" or "Have I ever loved the wrong thing?" Augustine thinks we will all answer, "yes!" At the third level, Augustine thinks we can know what is good, love what is good, and yet still find ourselves unable to per-form the good. To follow Augustine's basic position on this score, we should ask ourselves, "Have I ever known what was good and wanted to do it, but still found myself doing something else?" Again, Augustine thinks we will all answer, "yes!" For Augustine, this means that we are all in need of multiple kinds of grace.

EXEGESIS OF ORIGINAL SIN

The third chapter of Genesis means that all humans are broken ac-cording to Augustine. To say that we are broken is not to say that we are completely evil. For Augustine, evil does not have existence on its own; rather, evil is the perversion of good.[1] Here, he relies on a popular strain of thought that derives from Plato, the ancient Greek

---

1. See, e.g. Augustine, *Confessions* 7.11.17–7.16.22.

philosopher who was a disciple of Socrates. Augustine's point is that we only call something "broken" or "damaged" if it is obvious what good the thing was meant to do or is capable of doing. An amorphous pile of trash is not broken, but a hammer without a handle is. To use another image, consider a car with a broken starter motor. Most of us have the experience of relying on a car that has problems starting. Sometimes, it will start and take us where we need to go. But sometimes it will fail to start. We know we cannot rely on a broken car to function all the time, and so, we know that the car is bound to fail (usually at the worst possible moment). Augustine's sense of the brokenness of humanity is like that. It is not that we can never understand truth, never love the beautiful, and never do the good. Rather, broken humanity will not always understand every truth, will not unfailingly love the truly beautiful, and will not always do good. This brokenness belongs to humanity from the original sin of Adam and Eve in the Garden of Eden. Genesis 1 and 2 reveal that humanity is created good. Genesis 3 reveals that we pervert that goodness and then suffer the consequences. Augustine follows Paul in reading the universal significance of this original sin: "Through one man sin entered the world, and through sin death, and in that way it was passed on to all human beings."[2]

> *Original sin* can be used in two theological senses: 1) It refers to the first sin, which in Sacred Scripture is the sin of Eve and Adam in the Garden of Eden. 2) It refers to the Augustinian understanding of this first sin that entails the brokenness and guilt of all humans and the need for Christ's grace, which is normally offered in the sacrament of Baptism.

Why do we find ourselves in this state of brokenness? To use Paul's saying, why does the "flesh [have] desires against the Spirit, and the Spirit against the flesh . . . so that you may not do what you want?"[3] For Augustine the answer lies in Genesis 3. Things were near perfect for Adam and Eve in the Garden of Eden, but both Eve and Adam chose to disobey God's command not to eat of the

2. Rom 5:12 as translated in Augustine, *Gift of Perseverance* 12.30, trans. Teske in WSA 1.26.210.

3. Gal 5:17.

fruit of the tree of the knowledge of good and evil. In doing so, they disrupted human existence for all others and were banished from the Garden. "For Adam could fall willingly . . . but could not also rise up, and this misery of just condemnation includes the ignorance and difficulty which every human being suffers from the first moments of his birth."[4] Paul describes the state of fallen humans: "sin dwells in me. For I know that good does not dwell in me, that is, in my flesh. The willing is ready at hand, but doing the good is not. For I do not do the good I want, but I do the evil I do not want."[5] Augustine reflects "that it is not in our power to do that which is good is part of the deserts of original sin. This is not the original nature of man, but the penalty of his guilt."[6]

NECESSITY AND SUFFICIENCY FOR SALVATION

For Augustine, Heaven is not attainable without grace for two reasons. First, Heaven is beyond our abilities. We could never get there on our own human powers. Second, since we have damaged ourselves, we not only lack the ability to get to Heaven, but we also do not deserve God's help to arrive there. Since "all have sinned and are deprived of the glory of God," all humans are in need of God's grace in order to achieve heaven.[7] Jesus Christ offers this grace, and so, the grace of Christ is necessary for salvation. In fact, it is human insufficiency that demands divine necessity when it comes to salvation. Augustine argues staunchly that humans, in our fallen state, are not sufficient to attain salvation. Divine grace is necessary. Nearly all of Augustine's modern interpreters understand these two principles, human insufficiency and divine necessity. Augustine summarizes the points often, as when he wrote to two theologians who were puzzling over his teachings: "The human race is born subject to the sin of the first man [Original Sin]

---

4. Augustine, *Gift of Perseverance* 11.27, trans. Teske in WSA 1.26.207.

5. Rom 7:17–19.

6. Augustine, *To Simplician* 1.11, trans. J. Burleigh, 381.

7. Rom 3:23.

and . . . no one is set free from this evil except by the righteousness of the second man [necessity of grace through Christ] . . . No one is by himself sufficient for either beginning or carrying out any good work [human insufficiency]."[8]

In his own day, figures like Pelagius debated with Augustine and argued that at least some humans were sufficient on their own to earn Heaven. They taught that "we have faith from ourselves, but that its increase comes from God," when Augustine taught that "the faith by which we are Christians is a gift of God."[9] For them, grace could be a great aid in achieving heaven, but was not technically necessary. Augustine found that kind of teaching to be plainly in error. He argued that Scripture reveals human insufficiency and divine necessity in matters of salvation. "It is not . . . in the power of human beings, but in the power of God that humans have the *power to become children of God.*"[10] Grace is needed not only at the very beginning, but throughout Christian life even to the final moment of this life. "In order to receive and hold onto this good and to make progress in it with perseverance up to the end, we are not *sufficient to have a single thought as if from ourselves, but our sufficiency comes from God.*"[11] Augustine also argued that basic human experience reveals that we are frail, limited, and not sufficient to attain perfection on our own. Augustine firmly taught divine necessity and human insufficiency for salvation.

	God's Grace	Human Will
Augustine	Necessary	Necessary but Insufficient
Pelagius	Not Necessary	Necessary and Sufficient

8. Augustine, *Predestination of the Saints* 1.2, trans. Teske in WSA 1.26.149–150.

9. Ibid., 2.3, trans. Teske in WSA 1.26.150.

10. Augustine, *Gift of Perseverance* 8.20, trans. Teske in WSA 1.26.202, quoting John 1:12.

11. Ibid., quoting 2 Cor 3:5.

Even in Augustine's day and especially in modern times, readers of Augustine have taken human insufficiency and divine necessity to imply that there is no role for human efforts at all in salvation. They might articulate this as divine sufficiency (God alone) or as complete human inability (a doctrine called "total depravity"). Neither are Augustine's own position. Augustine, in fact, argues that humans do have a role to play in our own and others' salvation. "It is equally true that the mercy of God is not sufficient of itself, unless there be in addition the consent of our will. Clearly it is in vain for us to will unless God has mercy. But . . . if God has mercy, we also will, for the power to will is given with the mercy itself."[12] Thus, Augustine teaches human necessity in addition to divine necessity and human insufficiency when it comes to salvation. To put it another way, neither God nor the human are surprised to find the saint in Heaven. Both God and humans work toward human salvation and have roles to play in salvation history.

> The *total depravity* of humanity in the strongest sense means that humans can do nothing good without special grace from God.

DIVINE GRACE AND HUMAN WILL

Grace is the necessary antidote for original sin. If original sin means we do not always know what is good and true, then grace enables our minds to see truth clearly. If original sin means that we do not always love what is good, beautiful, and true, then grace frees our human will to love what is good, beautiful, and true. If original sin means that we sometimes know and want to do something, but find ourselves unable, then grace gives us that power to do what we should. Grace works within human nature to renew it to the original state found in Genesis 1 and 2, according to Augustine. Grace also elevates us beyond our normal human abilities so that we no longer even want to sin. Eventually, we are transformed and perfected so that it is no longer even possible to sin when we arrive in Heaven.

12. Augustine, *To Simplician* 2.12, trans. J. Burleigh, 394.

Augustine makes several complicated arguments about how divine grace works within human will. An overview is helpful so that we can pay special attention to his conclusion. According to Augustine, humans have a free will wounded and held captive by sin. Our ability to love or choose (free will) is not actually free due to original sin. We are, in effect, addicted to evil. Just as we do not think the addict is free from her addiction, Augustine does not think the sinner is truly free. It is sin that binds us and makes us slaves.[13] We often think that freedom means the ability to sin or not to sin, but this is not the way Augustine thinks about it. Again, to grasp the force of Augustine's view, we should think of whether we think of the addict as truly free, or whether we think of those not addicted as more free. Grace frees us from our addiction to sin. Grace liberates us from the captivity of sin. Thus, we are born with a free will that is nevertheless bound to sin, but we are reborn with a liberated free will that knows and loves the truth and beauty of God. Grace does not work against free will; nor does grace simply cover over free will, leaving it damaged on the inside. Rather, grace changes our very desire so that we no longer want evil. Instead of removing the drug (evil), but keeping the addiction to the drug, grace acts to remove the addiction itself. This is often a slow and painful process, but Augustine argues that God gives us different kinds of graces for each challenge along the way.

> Grace liberates human free will, which is otherwise bound by original sin.

Augustine was asked a series of questions by some fellow African monks concerning grace and free will. He summarized the debate in his response to them: "there are some who defend the grace of God so that they deny the free choice of human beings or who think that free choice is denied when grace is defended."[14] Augustine, of course, argues that neither option is the Christian one. Both grace and free will are needed. Christian salvation includes

---

13. See especially Rom 6 for some of the texts that resonate most deeply with Augustine on this line of thought.

14. Augustine, *Grace and Free Choice* 1.1, trans. Teske in WSA 1.26.71.

both faith and good works. One does not exclude the other, according to Augustine. "But there is reason to fear that [all of this] may be understood in the defense of free choice in such a way that for a pious life and good behavior, which merits an eternal reward, no place is left for the help and grace of God."[15] Christianity is not a theory of human free will to the exclusion of grace. Nor is it a theory of grace to the exclusion of human merit. "The grace of God is not given in accord with our merits . . . but . . . once grace has been given, our good merits also begin to exist."[16] Because the first major kind of grace we are given is faith, Augustine makes specific arguments about faith. Hope and love are also graces given by God, but faith is the first action of grace within our lives and merits special study. Augustine does not separate faith from good works as later theologians will attempt. "But people who did not understand . . . thought that . . . faith was enough for a man, even if he lives a bad life and does not have good works."[17] Rather, according to Galatians 5:6, "faith works through love," and Augustine argues "this is the faith which separates the faithful of God from the unclean demons."[18] Love is expressed in good works, and those good works merit eternal life. "Our good works . . . , for which eternal life is our recompense, also pertain to the grace of God."[19] Both divine grace and human wills are needed for salvation. This means that humans who arrive in Heaven deserve to be there. Grace transforms humans so that we can merit everlasting life.

Since Augustine argues that grace liberates human free will, there is no competition between divine grace and human will. We are often tempted to think of salvation in terms of competing agencies. We think that either God saves us and we do not, or we save ourselves and God does not. We force a split between God and humanity. Augustine argues no such split exists when it comes to the choice of love. Rather, God's grace enables us to

15. Ibid., 4.6, trans. Teske in WSA 1.26.75.
16. Ibid., 6.13, trans. Teske in WSA 1.26.79.
17. Ibid., 7.18, trans. Teske in WSA 1.26.82.
18. Ibid., 7.18, trans. Teske in WSA 1.26.82.
19. Ibid., 8.19, trans. Teske in WSA 1.26.83.

love properly. That is, when the Christian loves, the Christian loves with her own love, but that love has been enkindled by God. There is no competition between God and humans, but rather perfect union in love. Again, Christians are converted and reformed by grace into perfect lovers of God and neighbor. Those transformed by God's love become people who truly merit Heaven.

THE *MASSA DAMNATA*, HELL, AND GOD'S INSCRUTABLE WILL

Despite teaching that God's grace truly changes human lives, allowing us to love properly and merit eternal life, Augustine still argues that many people will arrive in Hell. Furthermore, unlike in Origen's speculation, Hell is "everlasting punishment of the damned" that includes "pain from the fires" that affects both humans and demons.[20] He seems to have inherited the idea that a large mass of people are damned from his fellow African Christians. The Latin phrase *massa damnata* and related terms had been popular from at least Cyprian of Carthage in the third century, and Augustine follows suite with its usage. The basic line of thought is easy to follow, but the conclusions are not as easy to swallow. If everyone has sinned and fallen short, as St. Paul and Genesis 3 teach, then everyone deserves Hell. No human can lay claim to deserve Heaven. If we think of the storyline of salvation up to Jacob and Esau, we see that Augustine argues that we basically find what we expect: people make mistakes with dire consequences and do not deserve Heaven. But sometimes it looks like people do good of their own accord and without God's help. It almost looks as if people earn Heaven on their own, as if we were sufficient to get ourselves to Heaven. When we get to Jacob and Esau, however, Augustine thinks he has clear proof that everyone deserves Hell and that God mysteriously saves some. The twins deserve the same punishment because there can be no distinction between them, and God pronounces judgment before they are born. We tend to

20. Augustine, *City of God* 21.9–10, trans. M Dodds, 778–780.

identify with Jacob and think God's hatred for Esau needs explanation. But for Augustine, we should expect God's hatred for Esau. Esau is, after all, a human born of the line of Adam who is broken and sinful. Due to original sin, both Jacob and Esau deserve Hell.[21] For Augustine, it's God's love of Jacob that needs explanation. God has absolutely no reason to love Jacob, and yet, God does. In fact, God redeems Jacob with his love. This is the mystery which needs exploration. This is the mystery we celebrate as Christians. This is the mystery Augustine thinks we can never fully understand because it is beyond our reason.

Sin is also never fully understood. Unlike God's love, however, sin is simply unintelligible in itself. We can expect that Esau will be a sinner and point to human fallen-ness, but we can never truly explain why anyone turns away from God's love. And yet, we are tempted to think that it is unfair for God to love Jacob to the point of redemption (something he does not deserve) and hate Esau to the point of damnation (something both he and Jacob deserve). We apply the same question about Jacob and Esau to our contemporaries. Why God eventually saves some, but not others vexes us, but Augustine argues it must continue to vex us. "If . . . I am asked why God who gave them the love by which they lived as Christians did not give them perseverance, I reply that I do not know."[22] We must "be content not to know . . . why God gives this to some and not to others," for "how inscrutable are [God's] judgments and unsearchable his ways."[23]

> *Massa damnata* is a Latin term used by many North African theologians to denote that humanity after the Fall is a mass of those condemned to sin and Hell. For Augustine, the doctrine of original sin implies that humanity is a *massa damnata*.

One of the most difficult verses of Scripture for Augustine's theory that many end up in Hell due to original sin is 1 Tim 2:3–4: "This is good and pleasing to God our savior, who wills [all] to be

21. This is quite different from the later Calvinist doctrine of double predestination. Compare, for example, Augustine, *Gift of Perseverance* 22.57–61.

22. Augustine, *Rebuke and Grace* 8.17, trans. Teske in WSA 1.26.119.

23. Ibid., 8.18, trans. Teske in WSA 1.26.119, quoting Rom 11:33.

saved and to come to knowledge of the truth." Augustine makes several attempts to read this verse and comes to focus on what "all" means. He argues that "we should understand all the predestined, because every kind of human being is contained in them."[24] "All" does not mean "each and every" person, but rather "some of every kind" of person. Augustine argues that there are other verses in Scripture which use "all" or "every" in the same limited sense, and thus, he has an exegetical argument in response to the more natural reading of the verse. Augustine wants to avoid the theory that God firmly wills that everyone be saved, but that some fickle humans are able to thwart God's will and bring themselves to Hell. That would mean that finite human will limits or overturns infinite divine will, and that is not acceptable. At the same time, Augustine wants to avoid the idea that God firmly chooses some for damnation. Many theologians think you cannot have it both ways, but Augustine attempts to make that argument. After the Fall, everyone deserves Hell; God freely predestines some to Heaven, and those predestined are genuinely converted to be good and holy lovers of God and neighbor.

RECEPTION OF AUGUSTINE

It is no exaggeration to say that Christian thought, especially Christian thought articulated in the Western (Latin) tradition which most Americans know simply as "Christianity," is shaped by Augustine.[25] Whether theologians agree or disagree, they nearly always respond to Augustine at one level or another. This is especially the case with Augustine's theology of love, grace, human will, and salvation. The difficult task in studying the reception of Augustine's thought is not so much *whether* later theologians engage Augustine, but rather *how* they do so. Later theologians disagree on who is a better reader of Augustine. It seems clear

24. Ibid., 14.44, trans. Teske in WSA 1.26.139.

25. There are many Eastern Christian traditions, as well, but most Christians in America are either Roman Catholic or Protestant, both of which are Western forms of Christianity.

that some of the theologians who first agree with Augustine are Augustinian in a way that later theologians are not. For example, councils of bishops that met in Augustine's own lifetime adopted many of his theological principles, and even his own formulations of doctrines. The bishops gathered in Carthage several times in Augustine's lifetime; he joined them on many occasions. Thus, it is no wonder that a council like the one held in Carthage in 418 largely adopted Augustine's understanding of salvation.[26] Other councils adopted Augustine's theology, perhaps by a less direct route, as with the council that met in Orange in 529 and provided numerous excerpts from his writings.[27] In many ways even the exceptionally famous councils like Trent and Vatican II still rely heavily on Augustine and could be considered "Augustinian."

There are other ways Augustine's theology is received, as with theologians like St. Prosper of Aquitaine, who attempt to absorb and apply Augustine's principles. Prosper wrote directly to Augustine while both were still alive and made every effort to understand and teach Augustine's theology, even if it took him some time to fully understand its complexities. Perhaps one of the greatest ways the influence of Augustine is made known in Prosper's work is in his articulation of the human will as having three levels: a natural level, a rational level, and a spiritual level.[28] The three levels correspond to the kind of grace that is given to the human person, but at all levels the will belongs firmly to the human agent so that God works with, in, and through humans; grace does not work against human nature. The "spiritual will" is completely alive with the Holy Spirit and loves with a divine love that can still be attributed to the human agent, for it is a human will elevated by God's grace. This tradition finds a particular zenith in the Scholastic discussions of cooperative grace and bears the popular slogan "grace perfects nature."

26. The texts of this council are translated in Burns, *Theological Anthropology* 57–60.

27. The texts of this council are translated in Burns, *Theological Anthropology* 109–128.

28. Prosper of Aquitaine, *Call of All Nations* 1.2–1.4. Scholars debate whether Prosper wrote this text, but no other author has gained the consensus opinion, and the text is published today under Prosper's name.

KEY QUESTIONS

Not all scholars agree on how we determine if someone is "Augustinian." In part this is because Augustine wrote so much and made so many arguments that we have to be selective with our criteria. For the sake of this short introduction, it is helpful to return to the same questions we posed of Origen's speculations. For Augustine, like Origen, humans are directly responsible not only for our present sins, but also for that initial or original sin that landed us where we find ourselves at the beginning of life in this world. However, unlike Origen, Augustine teaches that every other human was included in Adam and Eve's Fall. Their Fall causes the sinfulness of those who come after them. Origen taught that each rational will had a separate "original" sin. Still, like Origen, Augustine argues that human free will answers the problem of evil. Natural diversity is handled differently. Working from the creation accounts in Genesis 1 and 2, Augustine argues that God directly intends good diversity, but that the negative aspects of diversity stem from original sin. Like Origen, Augustine argues that God is not responsible for evil in any sense. Those who convert to God are definitely aided by God, but they make a free choice to love God. Thus, both God and humans are responsible for salvation.

Other questions that are worth reflection and discussion include:

- When we read that God loves Jacob and hates Esau, do we fixate on God's love or God's hate?

- Most of our contemporaries think of infants as innocent. Do we agree with Augustine that all humans (infants included) are at least broken from original sin? What does it mean to say that infants are guilty of sin?

- Does God's divine love for us remove or impinge on our human freedom?

- Does an addiction make one less free?

- Does love make one less free? (i.e. are lovers *obligated* to do things to which nonlovers are not obligated?)

- What does Genesis 3 imply for us today?

31

A SHORT CRITIQUE OF ST. AUGUSTINE

Augustine insists that original sin applies to all humans at least from birth. This means that infants are sinful in Augustine's account. That runs contrary to our modern sensibility that infants are innocent. Many find Augustine's teaching that original sin applies to infants and that grace through baptism in a specific Christian denomination is the only means to salvation problematic. What should be believed about infants who die before they could be baptized? Earlier in his life, Augustine considered the idea that perhaps God would judge such infants based on what they would have done had they lived long enough. God judges them on their future actions or merits (aka *"futurabilia"*). But Augustine comes to reject that notion because then God would choose some for Heaven based on their future merit and not based on his own grace. "God . . . did not in his foreknowledge choose the works of anyone . . . It is, of course, not grace if any merits come before it, for what is given, not as grace, but as something due, is a repayment for merits rather than a gift."[29] Those who consider infants to be innocent until they sin consciously as adolescents, critique Augustine on account of his doctrine of infant sin and the necessity for infant baptism. It seems unjust that infants who die before baptism would go straight to Hell.

Augustine came to think that salvation depends upon a grace that is freely given and is necessary for salvation. This appears to leave God negligent in the case of those who are never given that grace. A charitable reading of Augustine on original sin might get God off the hook for someone like Esau. Born under the sin of Adam and Eve, both Esau and Jacob deserve Hell. God is not unjust to save Jacob because Esau deserves what he gets. But this only pushes the problem back to *the* original sin of Adam and Eve, which ultimately remains inexplicable for Augustine. This leaves Augustine open to critique: it seems that his solution to the problem of evil is simply to say, "look, it happened in Genesis 3." Another significant critique of Augustine comes from the other end of salvation history. Augustine

29. Augustine, *Predestination of the Saints* 3.7, trans. Teske in WSA 1.26.153.

assumes that a great many will end up in Hell, even though he has all the tools needed to argue that everyone could go to Heaven. Augustine is a compatibilist between divine and human will; he argues that they work together and are not mutually exclusive. Augustine thinks that God can convert the sinner with a grace that is irresistible. This raises the question of why Augustine was committed to the belief that anyone goes to Hell when it seems that God could, in fact, give every fallen human the kind of grace that would ensure they all converted and persevered.

4

John Calvin and Double Predestination

John Calvin (1509–1564) was one of the most influential Protestant Reformers of the sixteenth century. He has earned the honor of being the fountainhead of the "Calvinist" denomination, much like the German Protestant theologian, Martin Luther, from whom we name the Lutherans. Like many Medieval theologians, Calvin was familiar with a lot of Augustine's thought and followed him in many respects. Calvin regularly defended the priority of grace, human insufficiency, and divine necessity in explaining his theory of salvation. Differing from Augustine, Calvin taught that Scripture alone was the way to truth. Further differing from Augustine, Calvin argued that Scripture teaches not only that God predestines some to Heaven, but also that God predestines the rest to Hell. This doctrine is often called the doctrine of "double predestination" because there are two different destinies that God determines for humans. "It is plainly owing to the mere pleasure of God that salvation is spontaneously offered to some, while others have no access to it . . . some [are] predestinated to salvation, and others to destruction."[1] In the final analysis, God alone is responsible both for those who go to Heaven and those who go to Hell. Thus, Calvin

1. Calvin, *Institutes* 3.21.1, trans. Beveridge, 2.202.

differs from earlier Christian theologians, who had argued for a distinction between predestination (which was always to Heaven) and reprobation (which was punishment in Hell deserved by human sin). Calvin presents a new school of thought with regard to a theory of Christian salvation. Calvin's most bold thesis is that this double predestination is chosen by God *prior to Creation* so that God creates some people specifically for damnation.

SCRIPTURE REVEALS THAT DOUBLE PREDESTINATION BELONGS TO GOD ALONE

Calvin constantly reminds his readers to be cautious when exploring God's plan of salvation and damnation. "When they inquire into predestination, let them remember that they are penetrating into the recesses of the divine wisdom, where he who rushes forward . . . will enter the inextricable labyrinth."[2] Calvin argues that Scripture reveals quite simply that "all are not created on equal terms, but some are preordained to eternal life, others to eternal damnation."[3] Furthermore, "few . . . out of the great number of the called are chosen."[4] When we consult Scripture, Calvin argues that the Old Testament points to God's selection of only a few people to belong to his covenant. Calvin concludes with an analysis of Paul quoting the prophet Malachi about Jacob and Esau. "Paul skillfully argues . . . that when God . . . invites any people to himself, a special mode of election is in part understood, so that he does not

> *Double Predestination* names John Calvin's theory that God predestines a few humans to Heaven and the majority of humans to Hell. Other theologians speak of predestination only to Heaven, and use other language (like "reprobation" or "judgment") to name God's relationship to those who choose Hell in order to note that God is not the cause of damnation.

2. Ibid., 3.21.1, trans. Beveridge, 2.204.
3. Ibid., 3.21.5, trans. Beveridge, 2.206.
4. Ibid., 3.24.8, trans. Beveridge, 2.206.

with promiscuous grace effectually elect all of them."[5] Furthermore, Calvin thinks Paul teaches that the number of the elect is smaller rather than larger. Arguing from the word *remnant* used in Rom 9:27 and 11:5, Calvin teaches "of the general body many fall away and are lost, so that often a small portion only remains."[6]

Like Augustine, Calvin teaches that God's election is not based on human merit, either past or future. Calvin argues that when we read Scripture, we see that in every case God's plan and God's action are prior to human actions. He follows Augustine in rejecting human merit (including *futurabilia* arguments) as the initial cause of grace. It is important for Calvin that God have free choice to give grace to whom he pleases. Salvation comes exclusively through God's grace (thus the popular slogan *sola gratia*—grace alone). Furthermore, according to Calvin this divine election is made prior to creation. This can lead to the "once saved, always saved" mentality that has been popularized in some parts of American Christianity. But Calvin rejects a superficial reading of divine election and the salvation that comes from it. "Election," he teaches, "does not give men any occasion for license. Impious people blaspheme, saying; 'let us live as we please . . . If we are elect, it is impossible that we should perish.'"[7] Calvin rejects that notion because if one is given grace, one should no longer sin flagrantly. Grace, in effect, prevents horrific sins. "It is vicious to separate the holiness of life from the grace of election."[8] If God chooses someone for salvation, God will also grant that person a sure faith and holiness. Thus, Calvin rejects that human will or action has any role to play in meriting salvation, but this does not mean that those who are saved could be bold sinners.

---

5. Ibid., 3.21.7, trans. Beveridge, 2.209.

6. Ibid., 3.21.7, trans. Beveridge, 2.209.

7. Calvin, *Commentaries* "On Election," trans. J. Haroutunian in *Library of Christian Classics*, 23.304.

8. Ibid., 23.304.

RESPONSIBILITY FOR (THE PROBLEM OF) EVIL

Like Origen, Calvin links his understanding of double predestination to his understanding of the problem of natural diversity. But very much unlike Origen, Calvin does not pin the solution on creaturely freedom. There is no attempt to answer the problem of evil by claiming that God is not responsible for the seeming unfairness of natural diversity or Adam's sin. Rather, Calvin acknowledges that double predestination is a difficult doctrine to accept. "It seems harsh to many to think that God chooses some and rejects others, and does not consider men's worth . . . If it is unreasonable for God to choose one of two men and reject the other, how can we defend God's justice in creating a donkey and a man—if it needs defense? For . . . the bodies of donkeys and men come from the same clay."[9] The thought experiment here is to imagine the soul of a donkey complaining that it was given life as a donkey instead of life as a human. This is ludicrous. The donkey should be grateful for being created and not complain about being a donkey. Beggars cannot be choosers, according to the popular saying. Similarly, Calvin argues it is ludicrous for the soul of a reprobate human to complain that she was given a life intended for Hell instead of a life intended for Heaven. Origen attempted to explain natural diversity by appeal to some kind of fundamental and prior choice made by rational creatures. Augustine never committed himself to Origen's theory.

> Double predestination implies that *God is responsible for good and for what we perceive as evil.*

Augustine did, however, attempt to answer the problem of evil by arguing that humans are directly responsible for evil in the Fall. Thus, both Origen and Augustine argue that creatures are responsible for their own negative situations and are the cause of evil. Calvin argues that God is directly responsible for such evils.

What is more, Calvin argues that God could give grace to all, but freely chooses not to do so. "The fact that not all receive the gospel is not due to the impotence of God, who could readily make

9. Ibid., 23.294.

all creatures submit . . . That some arrive at faith, while others remain stupefied and obstinate, is due to his free election."[10] The case is particularly stark with the Pharaoh of Moses' day, whose heart God hardened. Calvin argues that "God used Pharaoh as an example" in order to reveal the glory of his name.[11] God could have brought the Hebrew People out of Egypt without having to send the plagues upon Pharaoh and the Egyptian people, but He freely chose to harden Pharaoh's heart instead. Calvin argues that "it is wicked to construe this work of God as unjust."[12] Rather, whatever God does is, by definition, just. We would be wrong to question why God made this one a donkey, that one a reprobate human, and this one a saved human. In all cases, we would be wrong for the same reasons, according to Calvin. Creation is entirely dependent on God, and God is always just.

MAKING SENSE OF DOUBLE PREDESTINATION

Calvin does speak of original sin in ways that remind us of Augustine. Calvin speaks of original sin and the *massa damnata*, though this suggests a kind of total depravity to do good for Calvin. Like Augustine, Calvin teaches that we should not focus on those who are reprobate. Somewhat unlike Augustine, Calvin teaches that we should simply accept our position with respect to God's will. Augustine always held out that one could convert or deny Christ before death, and so, nothing was certain in this life. Augustine also taught that humans were responsible for their own sin; Calvin flatly disagrees: "I admit that by the will of God all the sons of Adam fell into that state of wretchedness in which they are now involved . . . but we must always return to the mere pleasure of the divine will, the cause of which is hidden in himself."[13] The will of God is not to be questioned, nor is it to be limited in any sense by our notion of what

10. Ibid., 23.296.

11. Ibid., 23.301.

12. Ibid., 23.301.

13. Calvin, *Institutes* 3.23.4, trans. Beveridge, 2.229.

would constitute a good, loving, or just God. In fact, Calvin argues that "the will of God is the supreme rule of righteousness, so that everything which he wills must be held to be righteous by the mere fact of his willing it."[14] This emphasis on the divine will is one of two ways Calvin helps his readers make sense of what otherwise seems like an unacceptable doctrine of double predestination. It is not that God wills something evil or awkward; that would be to judge God's will from the perspective of what we think is evil or awkward. Rather, God's will defines justice. As long as we focus on God's will as the source of what is just, it does not seem unfair that God would create some humans for eternal damnation. By definition, whatever God wills is fair and just, including the creation of many for eternal damnation.

> For Calvin, God's divine will defines all other categories. We should not question it.

A second major theme for Calvin in making sense of double predestination is the glory of God. All things should work towards the greater glory of God. As Calvin teaches, "the highest and ultimate purpose of election . . . is that we glorify God."[15] Both the salvation of a few and the damnation of many demonstrate the power and glory of God for Calvin. This is almost the exact reverse of Origen, who argued that the power and glory of God was best shown by his ability to eventually *restore* all things. For Calvin, God's power and glory are revealed in saving some and damning others. God displays his "free goodness" by saving a few and "to display his own glory, withholds from [the condemned] the effectual agency of his Spirit."[16]

> For Calvin, it serves the glory of God for some humans to go to Hell and others to go to Heaven.

14. Ibid., 3.23.2, trans. Beveridge, 2.227.

15. Calvin, *Commentaries* "On Election," trans. J. Haroutunian in *Library of Christian Classics*, 23.306.

16. Calvin, *Institutes* 3.23.2, trans. Beveridge, 2.227.

PROOF OF ELECTION

The existential and emotional situation of a Christian fascinated Calvin. Just as he argued forcefully that one could not be eternally elected by God and continue to be a profligate sinner, Calvin argued that the elect gain a sense of their own election. To be sure, the plan of salvation is hidden in the mystery of God, and we should never presume to know someone else's salvation. If, however, we feel the work of the Holy Spirit within, we have a sign that we are chosen and need not fear eternal damnation. "This inward calling is an infallible pledge of salvation."[17] It will be attacked by Satan, who disquiets believers "with doubts as to their election."[18] In fact, Calvin taught that one could get stuck asking whether one was chosen by God or not. Such a question "keeps [the believer] perpetually miserable, subjects him to dire torment, or throws him into a state of complete stupor."[19] In answer, Calvin counsels that we should remember salvation is offered in Christ alone and "those whom Christ enlightens with the knowledge of his name and admits into the bosom of his church, he is said to take under his guardianship and protection."[20] If we have belief in Christ, then this should be taken as a sign of our election. Those who seem to belong to the Church and then fall away "never adhered to Christ with heartfelt confidence."[21] They have always been among the reprobate, those God predestined for Hell.

KEY QUESTIONS

It is helpful to return to the same questions we posed of Origen's and Augustine's thought. These reveal that Calvin differs from Augustine on one significant point. For Augustine and Origen, humans are directly responsible for sin. Calvin agrees that humans

17. Ibid., 3.24.2, trans. Beveridge, 2.242.
18. Ibid., 3.24.4, trans. Beveridge, 2.243.
19. Ibid., 3.24.4, trans. Beveridge, 2.243.
20. Ibid., 3.24.6, trans. Beveridge, 2.245.
21. Ibid., 3.24.7, trans. Beveridge, 2.246.

are culpable, but it is God's will that Adam and Eve sinned according to Calvin. Thus, Calvin has a different answer to the problem of evil and natural diversity. God directly intends both the natural diversity that we observe today and the evil in the world that stems from Adam and Eve's original sin. Those born into poverty were made intentionally for that poverty. Those who end up in Hell were created specifically for Hell. Calvin's response to the problem of evil is that it is not a problem because we cannot judge God. Rather, we must trust that God's will defines justice. Calvin teaches that those who convert are necessarily aided by God, much like Augustine and Origen. Thus, for Calvin, divine grace is necessary, but God is cause of both good and bad in human lives.

Other questions that are worth reflection and discussion include:

- Is it soothing to think that all things (good and bad) work to the greater glory of God?

- Can we make sense of a Christian God who creates some humans for eternal damnation?

- Is double predestination compatible with human free will?

A SHORT CRITIQUE OF CALVIN

The major difficulty with Calvin's theory of double predestination was already known to him. It seems inconsistent with Christianity that God would willfully create many humans specifically for the purpose of eternal damnation. Calvin's response is to shift the primary perspective from the goodness and beauty of God to the will of God. The will of God is taken to be absolute and defines the other categories like goodness, truth, and beauty. Similarly, while it is easy for many to see how the salvation of some reveals the glory of God, it is difficult to see how the damnation of many reveals the glory of God. A second round of critique of double predestination wonders if it allows for any sense of human freedom. It is difficult to see how Calvin can make much room for genuine *human* freedom and free will when so much emphasis is placed on *divine* freedom and free will. The Augustinian reflection on love seems foreign to Calvin. Where Augustine announces and resolves a problem of competing agencies by arguing that there is no competition between lovers, Calvin argues that God remains the fundamental cause of both good and evil in human lives. Where Augustine reflects on how grace transforms the believer into a lover of God and neighbor who deserves Heaven, Calvin rejects that human merit has any role to play in salvation. That we have no role to play in our own salvation seems inconsistent with Christianity to many believers.

5

Hans Urs von Balthasar and
The Hope for Universal Salvation

IN MANY WAYS HANS Urs von Balthasar (1905–1988) led a life of
extremes. He became a Jesuit priest, but had to leave in order to
remain active as a leader of a new religious society. Discredited
as a teacher of theology, he was eventually appointed to the In-
ternational Theological Commission, which is a very prestigious
panel of theologians within the Catholic Church. A simple priest
throughout his life, he was appointed to become a Cardinal by
Pope John Paul II, but he died before the ceremony. Without a
doubt, Balthasar is one of the most erudite theologians of the
twentieth century, and his ideas are not without considerable
controversy. Perhaps that controversy is nowhere more bitter than
when focused on his understanding of salvation and, especially,
Hell. Balthasar defended the thesis that Christians should *hope* for
the salvation of every human, and even fallen angels.

THE EXEGETICAL PROBLEM REALLY IS A
PROBLEM

The standard solutions to the exegetical problem concerning salvation essentially select one set of biblical verses and privileges them

over the other. Either we follow Origen in thinking the promises of universal salvation are fundamental, or we follow Augustine in thinking the references to the eternal damnation of some are fundamental. In either case, the other set of biblical verses present a problem. Origen has to explain why Scripture would speak of some in Hell. His basic answer is to assume that Hell is remedial and has an end. Jacob goes straight to Heaven in God's love. Esau goes to Heaven by way of Hell because he needs God's hate to help him convert. Augustine has to explain why Scripture would speak of Christ as a universal savior and why God would will that all come to truth and be saved. His basic strategy is to attack the "all" and argue that it does not mean "each and every," but rather "some of every kind." The other arm of his strategy is to make humans responsible for our own downfall and then to argue that God has different kinds of grace that respond to different human situations. Balthasar argues that reading one set of verses over and against the other as though the one offers deeper insight than the other is a mistake. We must simply accept that no positive articulation of the matter is possible for us in this life. But this means that he must also work to show how one set of verses does not somehow prevent us from *hoping* in the other set of verses.

The exegetical argument Balthasar employs makes the obser-vation that both the thesis (of someone like Origen) that all will eventually be saved and the thesis (of someone like Augustine) that only some are saved are genuinely revealed in Scripture. Balthasar admits both types of passages. "In the new Testament, two series of statements run along side by side . . . the first series speaks of being lost for all eternity; the second of God's will, and ability, to save all men."[1] He rejects the move that Origen, Augustine, and Calvin entertain. He argues that we cannot privilege one set of verses over the other and then work to resolve the tension. "A synthesis of both is neither permissible nor achievable."[2] Balthasar does not attempt to solve the exegetical problem, but rather observes that the ex-egetical problem itself is the important datum. Once we observe

1. Balthasar, *Dare We Hope*, trans. Kipp & Krauth, 29.
2. Ibid., 29.

the exegetical problem, we realize no solution is possible for us in this life. Two different things are revealed to humans in such a way that our reason cannot reconcile or synthesize them. Balthasar concludes that God does not want us to work out a solution, but instead to observe the problem and leave it with no resolution.

No solution is possible for us in this life because we are *under judgment* in this life. The plan of salvation has not been worked out in our lives in time. Being under judgment in this life implies that "by no means are we above it, so that we might know its outcome in advance and could proceed from that knowledge to further speculation."[3] Since we are under judgment and there is an unsolvable exegetical problem, we cannot attempt to answer the exegetical problem as a matter of faith. Thus, "the question arises of just what form and scope Christian hope may, or may not, take."[4]

HOPING IS NOT BELIEVING

Critics of Balthasar argued that his claim that Christians should *hope* for all to be saved was the same thing as positively *affirming* that all will be saved. Critics also argued since the Church teaches we cannot *affirm* universalism, the Church also teaches that we cannot *hope* for universalism. Balthasar specifically denied that *hope* for universal salvation transgressed the long–standing prohibition against *affirming* universal salvation. Recall that in response to Origen, the Church proclaimed that it is wrong simply to affirm that every human will be saved and it is wrong to say that Hell will have an end. For Balthasar, however, there is a difference between hope and certainty. In this way Balthasar offers a critique of the basic methodology and assumptions of the majority of theologians who came before him. Most think we must answer the question "who is saved" as a matter of faith, knowledge, and certainty. A formal doctrine that pertains to the faith is taken to offer certainty. For example, the Trinity is a formal doctrine pertaining to the

3. Ibid., 13.
4. Ibid., 14.

faith. Christians argue that we are not wrong to call and think of God as Father, Son, and Spirit, three co-equal and irreducible persons in one Godhead. This attains a kind of certainty that differs from hope. Furthermore, if someone were to attempt to hope for a fourth person of the Trinity, Christian theologians would argue that such a hope is not possible. We are certain that God is Trinity, no more and no less. When we ask the question "how many are saved?" or "who is saved?" as a matter of faith, the answer first appears to have three possibilities: either everyone is saved, some are and some are not saved, or no one is saved. There are, in effect, only two options since no Christian theologian would accept that no one is saved. Theologians wrestle with these other two options under the virtue of faith. We expect a doctrine, then, either that everyone is saved or that only some are saved. On those terms, the main possibilities appear to be found in the teachings of Origen (asserting Universalism), Augustine (asserting that some are saved by God's authority and others are damned by their own sinfulness), and Calvin (asserting that some are saved by God, while others are damned by God). Balthasar, however, argues that we cannot answer the question under the virtue of faith with a firm doctrine. It is impossible to state a belief that decides whether all or some are saved. However, the impossibility of stating a doctrine of faith does not exclude the possibility of stating a hope. "How can anyone equate hoping with knowing? I hope that my friend will recover from his serious illness–do I therefore know this?"[5] Thus, Balthasar rejects the entire project of attempting to determine an answer to the question of salvation. No answer to the question "how many are saved?" is possible in this life because no belief about this is revealed in Scripture in a way that human reason can understand it. Theologians are wrong to try to answer this question under the virtue of faith, as though we could determine a belief about whether everyone or only a few are saved.

5. Ibid., 166.

HELL

The exegetical problem we have been tracing seems to suggest that one could not hope for the salvation of all because it has been revealed that at least some arrive in Hell. Augustine and Calvin both teach that many people have already arrived in Hell and many more will end up there for the rest of their afterlives. Even Origen admitted that some go to Hell, though they do not stay there for the duration of their afterlife. Belief in a populated Hell is also the way many of Balthasar's critics took the meaning of the exegetical problem. Against this, Balthasar makes three important claims. The first we have already noted: hope is not certainty. The majority of Balthasar's argument rests on whether we accept the distinction between doing theology under the virtue of faith (which allows for some articulation of certainty in doctrines) and doing theology under the virtue of hope (which avoids certainty in articulation of doctrine). The second is to argue that the Church has never definitively taught that a particular person is in Hell. On the other hand, the Church positively teaches that certain humans are in Heaven. Every saint the Church proclaims and venerates is a celebration of salvation. But the Church simply never proclaims a specific person in Hell.[6] Not even Judas must be believed to have gone to Hell, according to Balthasar's argument. The third main point is closely tied to the second. All references to Hell are meant to be didactic threats. They amount to saying "do not go there!" They are not meant to teach us that *this specific person* mentioned in the story is there. That is, passages about Hell in Scripture present the real threat of damnation. Balthasar questions whether "the transition from the threat to the *knowledge* that it will be carried out [is] necessary."[7] He argues it is not necessary, and where "certainty cannot be attained . . . hope can be justified."[8] Balthasar argues that these stories function similarly to when a parent tells a child, "Do not wreck the car, or else you will never drive again." The parent

6. E.g. Balthasar, *Dare We Hope,* trans. Kipp & Krauth, 164 & 187.

7. Ibid., 183.

8. Ibid., 187.

is not proclaiming that the child will wreck the car. We would be wrong to conclude from the threat a belief that the child will never drive again. Rather, we should conclude from the threat that the child should be very careful when driving. In fact, we should *hope* that the child *will not* wreck the car. Similarly, we should not conclude that people are in Hell, but rather develop a hope that everyone avoids the punishment specified in the threat.

When reflecting on Hell, Balthasar makes an astute point that combines spirituality with technical distinctions in theology. He argues that Hell is not a reflection for me about someone else, but rather a reflection for me about myself. I would be wrong to focus on Hell as a place for others. If I "begin to ponder on how many perish in . . . hell . . . woe is me if, looking back, I see how others, who were not so lucky as I, are sinking beneath the waves."[9] This kind of reflection on Hell for others makes us like the publican in Luke's Gospel who inappropriately prays "God, I thank [you] that I am not like other men . . . "[10] In fact, Balthasar argues, "whenever one fills hell with a '*massa damnata*' of sinners, one also . . . places oneself on the other side [in Heaven]."[11] Balthasar's critique of those who would fight for a doctrine that some are in Hell is that they have made Hell out to be a place for others. Hell is not a place for others, however; Hell is meant to be a meditation for me about my own faults and my own life with or without God. The point of teachings about Hell, according to Balthasar, is for me to avoid going to Hell. The point of teachings about Hell is not for me to figure out which of my neighbors will go there. There is much to take to heart in this argument.

OBLIGATORY HOPE

With the theological pathway cleared to allow the *possibility* of hope for the salvation of all, Balthasar closes his argument with a

9. Ibid., 190.

10. Luke 18:11, quoted in Balthasar, *Dare We Hope*, trans. Kipp & Krauth, 190.

11. Ibid., 191.

line of questioning about whether one *should* hope for the salvation of others. His conclusion is that Christians are obligated to hope for the salvation of everyone else. Balthasar notes that he is not referring to hope in an "easy" salvation for others in which the believer can sit back and let God work some special magic for other people. Rather, a genuine hope for others commits Christians to missionary activity in which those who already know God, have been Baptized in Christ, and are faithful Christians work to introduce others to Christ and bring them into the Church. Balthasar makes another theologian's words his own, and notes that "'heaven for all' does not mean something like an inducement to laziness in our ethical commitment but rather the heaviest demand upon all of us that one can imagine . . . If, on the basis of God's universal goodness, I cannot write anyone off for all eternity, then my eternal misfortune could consist precisely in the fact that I myself simply do not find the patience to wait infinitely long for the 'conversion of the other.'"[12] Genuine love of neighbor does not allow the Christian to hope for her damnation or abandon the possibility of the salvation of her neighbor.

KEY QUESTIONS

Because Balthasar rejects the basic premise of the debates between Origen, Augustine, and Calvin, he does not tie his theory of salvation to the problem of evil. Rather, he argues that his understanding of hope does not fall under important theological condemnations from the Church. Thus, Balthasar argues that hope for the salvation of all does not deny belief in Hell, though it does require that one argue Hell is not filled with people. Still, it is difficult to apply our standard questions to Balthasar when his point is that the exegetical problem has no solution, at least it has no solution while we are under judgment in this life.

---

12. H. Verweyen, *Christologische Brennpunkte*, 119–122, translated and quoted in Hans Urs von Balthasar, *Dare We Hope*, trans. Kipp & Krauth, 212.

Other questions that are worth reflection and discussion include:

- What are we to make of Sacred Scripture when it seems to contradict itself (i.e. with passages about people not being saved and passages about everyone being saved)?

- Does hoping for someone's salvation deny that person some sense of freedom (perhaps to choose Hell)?

- Can we meaningfully teach someone to hope in something without also teaching her to affirm it (i.e. to *hope* for universalism, but not *affirm* universalism)?

- Does Christianity require in any way that we believe that someone is in Hell?

A SHORT CRITIQUE OF BALTHASAR

The vast majority of Balthasar's argument rests on the intellectual move to separate hope from faith and the fact that the Church has never declared a particular person to be in Hell. Both can be questioned. It is, of course, true that we can and should make distinctions between the theological virtues of faith, hope, and love. But it seems inconsistent that one could say one thing under the virtue of hope and a contradictory thing under the virtue of faith. That is, even if we allow a distinction between what theology under hope might be able to do and what theology under faith might be able to do, we would not easily allow the two theological projects to disagree. If one admits the distinction between hope and faith, or if one admits the exegetical problem cannot be resolved while we are under judgment, the historical claim about what the Church has taught concerning Hell still remains. That is, were the Church to have claimed doctrinally under the virtue of faith that Judas is in Hell, it would seem impossible to hope for the salvation of Judas in just the same way that it would seem impossible to expect to find Mary the Mother of God in Hell, despite proclaiming her the Queen of Heaven as a matter of faith. There is ample evidence that many saints and doctors of the Church have taught that specific people are in Hell. Even the Gospels present evidence like the story of the rich man and Lazarus, in which the rich man ends up in Hell (Luke 16:19–31). Balthasar is open to critique in arguing that all such stories are meant to be parables for the individual to reflect on the real possibility of personal eternal damnation, but do not imply that the rich man is actually in Hell.

Conclusion

THERE ARE MORE THAN four significant theorists of Christian salvation. In the ancient world there are many who reflect on more extensive networks of Scriptural passages and theories about the divine nature. In the Medieval discussions we find deeper explorations of the causes of predestination and grace than we have been able to articulate here. Karl Rahner's notion that everyone, or at least most people, are "anonymously Christian" (that is, they are members of the Christian Church without knowing it) has been popular in modern conversations. The positions articulated by the Second Vatican Council are still being unpacked. There are also important dialogues to be considered, as with the Catholic–Lutheran dialogue and texts like the *Joint Declaration on Justification*. The role of the Church in salvation is crucial and plays a significant role in contemporary discussions of Christianity, but I have not introduced the ecclesial dimension of salvation which connects salvation to membership in a church. Though they mean different things by "church," all four considered here agree that salvation includes membership in the Church. Still, a short introduction to four theories of salvation serves us well as we sort through our own commitments and beliefs and attempt to square them with historical Christianity.

Conclusion

The terms of the debates about Christian salvation seem to be laid out quite precisely for contemporary Catholic theologians and those committed to decisions made over the centuries by councils of bishops. One must preserve the exclusive power of Christ as savior. One must also be committed to the Church as the means of salvation.[1] One must also preserve the absolute priority of grace in salvation while still maintaining that humans have free will. Furthermore, Hell is taught to be everlasting, definitive, immediate upon death, and even eternal.[2] In short, it seems that the modern Catholic theologian must explore this territory only while maintaining that God indeed has a plan for salvation which can properly be called "predestination," and that humans maintain freedom to love with the real possibility of separating ourselves from God.

The shape of the modern problem seldom follows the form of the exegetical problem we have traced here. Modern thinkers need to reflect deeply on the exegetical problem and historical responses to it. At the same time, the modern articulation of problems concerning salvation often takes the form of concern for those who are well outside the visible Church. We worry about the salvation of those who have never heard of Christ or seen the Gospels. In this regard, Balthasar's solution to both the problem as an exegetical puzzle and the possibility of salvation for those who never seem to have a chance to join the Christian Church is astute. The problem, strictly speaking, is not one for us to solve, but rather to observe. For many, it is not only possible, but also healthy to take refuge in the kind of silence his *hope for all* offers. When we worry about the salvation of others, Balthasar reminds us of two points. First, concern for others should impel us to missionary activity; we should work to convert all sinners to the Christian faith. Second, concern over damnation should be aimed at myself, and not at others. The plan of salvation is, in the end, something for me to work out with fear and trembling in hope that I, too, can play a

---

1. This is the doctrine of "outside the Church there is no salvation," repeated throughout the centuries to today, e.g. *Catechism of the Catholic Church* 846–48, *Unitatis Redintigratio* 3, and *Dominus Iesus* 20.

2. *Catechism of the Catholic Church* 1033–37.

role in the salvation of everyone else and myself. The plan of salvation is not some game I play from an armchair that includes judging my enemies and articulating how they end up suffering in Hell for eternity, while at the same time letting myself and my friends off easily. True conversion, both for myself and for others, is required. Where I cannot know about the salvation of others or even myself, I must remain silent and maintain hope in God's mercy. This Balthasarian reflection should encourage a deep respect for the unknowable aspects of the mystery of God and God's plan for salvation. But for many contemporary theologians it is impossible to remain silent. For those, it seems to me that Augustine provides helpful theological insight.

Calvin's God who predestines many humans directly to Hell and then creates them for that purpose in order to reveal his glory and Origen's speculation that Hell is temporary are off the table for Catholics. Augustine, however, is in the center of our theological tradition. Furthermore, for those concerned with the salvation of those outside the Church, Calvin's answer that they are simply predestined to Hell is unsatisfactory. Similarly, if reflection on Origenism allows us to be lazy and suppose that others are saved no matter what they do, we forfeit genuine human freedom and our role in the plan of salvation. If those same others are saved because they somehow express a non–Christian goodness or niceness, we have given up on Christianity's belief in the priority of grace and the necessity of Christ. If, on the other hand, it was possible to remove the belief that some go to Hell from Augustine's understanding of grace and free will, it seems that we would be left with a powerful understanding of the divine plan for salvation that might allow us to consider the salvation of those we do not currently recognize as part of the Church. God would bring them all into his mystical body by the same grace that converts any sinner. The sketch of that system would look like the following.

God initially created humanity with original goodness, but with the possibility of falling away from that goodness. Moreover, God made us for an even better state that we could only achieve in a deep and abiding relationship with him. Nevertheless, we did turn from him (the "Fall"), and this original sin has severe consequences. After the Fall, even though the conditions of human nature have changed such that we are wounded and in need of grace, God continues to love us not only with that love that restores us and liberates us to our original goodness and freedom, but God also loves us with that love which completes the relationship with him. The Church possesses the ministry of forgiveness of sins and reconciliation. The gates of Hell will not prevail against Christ's Church, and through her, humans can come to salvation. Because grace is not some forensic or legal mechanism, but rather the expression of God's love poured out in our hearts through the Holy Spirit (Rom 5:5), there is no competition between God's will and a mature human will. Liberated and restored, the human free will wants what God wants, namely to love God and neighbor perfectly. Even though God's love and beauty are irresistible, the divine will does not close down or shut off human freedom. God draws the will as a lover, not by force, but by the attraction of truth and beauty. All that is needed within this Augustinian framework is to ponder whether God reveals his irresistible truth and beauty to everyone before she dies, incorporating her into the Body of Christ, liberating her and empowering her to be a genuine lover of God and neighbor. Prayerful reflection on the transformative power of God's love is more Augustinian than reflection on the sterility of sin or the tragic refusal of redemption offered through Christ's Church. Those concerned with the salvation of others ought to be motivated by the same concern they have for their own salvation and work it out with fear and trembling, hoping that God will work in us to become blameless and innocent children of God who belong to the body of his son. (Phil 2:12–15)

Bibliography

Augustine. *City of God (civ. Dei)*. Translated by M. Dodds. Modern Library. New York, NY: Random House, 1993.

Confessions (Conf.). Translated by M. Boulding. Works of Saint Augustine 1.1. New York, NY: New City Press, 2001.

———. *Gift of Perseverance (dono pers.)*. Translated by R. Teske. Works of Saint Augustine 1.26. New York, NY: New City Press, 1999.

———. *Grace and Free Choice (grat. et lib. arb.)*. Translated by R. Teske. Works of Saint Augustine 1.26. New York, NY: New City Press, 1999.

———. *Predestination of the Saints (praed. sanct.)*. Translated by R. Teske. Works of Saint Augustine 1.26. New York, NY: New City Press, 1999.

———. *Rebuke and Grace (corr. et grat.)*. Translated by R. Teske. Works of Saint Augustine 1.26. New York, NY: New City Press, 1999.

———. *To Simplician (ad Simpl.)*. Translated J. Burleigh. *Augustine: Earlier Writings*. Philadelphia, PA: Westminster Press, 1953.

von Balthasar, Hans Urs. *Dare We Hope that All Men be Saved? With a Short Discourse on Hell*. Translated by Kipp & Krauth. San Francisco, CA: Ignatius Press, 1988.

Calvin, John. *Commentaries*. Translated by Joseph Haroutunian. Library of Christian Classics, 23. Philadelphia, PA: Westminster Press, 1958.

———. *Institutes of the Christian Religion*. Translated by H. Beveridge in 2 volumes. Reprint, Grand Rapids, MI: Eerdmans, 1994.

Catechism of the Catholic Church. Vatican: Libreria Editrice Vaticana, 1994.

Nicene and Post Nicene Fathers. 2 series with 28 volumes. Edited by Phillip Schaff. Grand Rapids, MI: Eerdmans,1886–1900.

Origen. *On First Principles (De Prin.)*. Translated by G. W. Butterworth. Reprint Eugene, OR: Wipf & Stock, 2012.